Opossums

by Sally M. Walker

Lerner Publications Company • Minneapolis

The photographs in this book are used with the permission of: © Maslowski Productions, pp. 4, 8, 10, 11, 12, 22, 23, 30, 33, 37, 38, 43; © Steve Maslowski/Visuals Unlimited, pp. 6, 26; © FLPA/Alamy, p. 7; © John Cancalosi/Peter Arnold, Inc., p. 9 (left); © Mark Hamblin/Oxford Scientific Films/Photolibrary, pp. 9 (right), 13; © Lynn M. Stone/naturepl.com, p. 14; © Steve Maslowski/Visuals Unlimited/Getty Images, pp. 15, 32; © Rolf Nussbaumer/Alamy, p. 16; © Greg Vaughn/Alamy, p. 17; © Gary Randall/Visuals Unlimited, p. 18; © Gay Bumgarner/Alamy, p. 19; © David Newman/Visuals Unlimited, p. 20; © Jeffrey Lepore/Photo Researchers, Inc., p, 21; © Joe McDonald/Visuals Unlimited, p. 24; © Kenneth M. Highfill/Photo Researchers, Inc., p. 25; © Leonard Lee Rue III/Visuals Unlimited, p. 27; © Konrad Wothe/Minden Pictures, pp. 28, 35; © Mary Mcdonald/npl/Minden Pictures, p. 29; © Garry Walter/Visuals Unlimited, pp. 31, 36, 48 (top); age fotostock/SuperStock, pp. 34, 39, 47; © Jack Milchanowski/Visuals Unlimited, p. 40; © Howard Stapleton/Alamy, p. 41; © Kitchin & Hurst/leesonphoto, p. 42; © SuperStock, Inc./SuperStock, p. 46; © Mark Graf/Alamy, p. 48 (bottom).

Front Cover: © Ethan Meleg/All Canada Photos/Getty Images
Illustration on p. 5 by © Laura Westlund/Independent Picture Service

Lerner Publications Company
A division of Lerner Publishing Group, Inc.
241 First Avenue North
Minneapolis, MN 55401 U.S.A.

Website address: www.lernerbooks.com

Library of Congress Cataloging-in-Publication Data

Walker, Sally M.
    Opossums / by Sally M. Walker.
       p.   cm. — (Early bird nature books)
    Includes index.
    ISBN 978–0–8225–3055–8 (lib. bdg. : alk. paper)
    1. Opossums—Juvenile literature. I. Title.
QL737.M34W35 2008
599.2'76—dc22   2007019775

Manufactured in the United States of America
1 2 3 4 5 6 – JR – 13 12 11 10 09 08

Contents

ALASKA (USA)

CANADA

N

UNITED STATES

Opossums (uh-PAH-sums) live in many places. The striped areas show where opossums live in North America.

MEXICO

Be a Word Detective

Can you find these words as you read about the opossum's life? Be a detective and try to figure out what they mean. You can turn to the glossary on page 46 for help.

carrion
dens
habitats
litter

marsupials
marsupium
nocturnal
opposable toe

predators
prehensile
wean

Chapter 1

This furry animal is an opossum. Where does the name opossum *come from?*

The Opossum

The sun sets. The leaves on a bush start to rustle. A pointy nose pokes through the leaves. It sniffs the nighttime air. Suddenly a furry animal scoots from under the bush. It is an opossum.

The name *opossum* comes from the Native American word *apasum*. This word means "white animal." But only the opossum's face is white. Its fur is mostly gray or black.

Opossums have white faces and grayish fur.

Opossums belong to a group of animals called marsupials (mahr-SOO-pee-uhls). Kangaroos and koalas are marsupials too. Female marsupials have a pouch on their bellies. They carry their babies in the pouch.

Opossums are the only marsupials that live in North America.

There are many different kinds of opossums. Most of them live in South America. Only one kind of opossum lives in North America. It is called the Virginia opossum. Let's take a look at the Virginia opossum.

Groups of animals called possums live in Australia. The animal on the left is a possum. The animal on the right is a Virginia opossum. Notice that these animals do not look the same.

Virginia opossums are 2 to 3 feet long. They weigh between 4 and 15 pounds. That is about the size of a cat.

Virginia opossums are about as big as cats. Opossums also climb trees like cats.

An opossum's sharp claws allow it to hold tightly to trees and other objects.

Virginia opossums have five toes on each front foot. Each toe has a sharp claw. An opossum's back feet also have five toes. But only four of those toes have sharp claws.

The fifth toe is larger than the others. It is called an opposable (uh-POH-zuh-buhl) toe. Opposable toes can hold on to things, just as a person's thumb can.

Virginia opossums have two layers of fur. The outer layer is thick and bristly. It is usually grayish white. The inner layer is soft. It is white tipped with black.

An opossum's thick, gray white fur hides a shorter layer of fur. The shorter layer is softer than the coarse outer layer.

This opossum has a pinkish tail.

Opossums' ears and tails are almost hairless. The Virginia opossum's ears look like leather. Its tail is scaly. It is whitish yellow or pink.

Opossums are good climbers. An opossum often walks on tree branches or narrow ledges. It waves its tail from side to side. This helps the opossum keep its balance.

Opossums' tails help keep the animals from falling off narrow tree branches.

Baby opossums sometimes hang upside down by their tails. Adult opossums do not normally do this. Their bodies are too heavy.

An opossum's tail is prehensile (pree-HEHN-suhl). This means that the tail can wrap around an object. An opossum can grab a branch with its tail. It can use its tail to help it climb trees.

Chapter 2

Opossums are nocturnal (nahk-TUHR-nuhl) animals. What does nocturnal *mean?*

Nighttime Hunters

Many animals sleep at night. But opossums are nocturnal. Nocturnal animals sleep in the daytime. They are active when the sun goes down.

Nighttime is when opossums hunt. Opossums spend much of the night looking for food.

Opossums hunt in bushes, trees, and even garbage cans. They often have to climb to find food. Opossums' claws, toes, and tails help them climb to high places.

Opossums can see well in the dark. Their good sense of sight helps them to hunt at night.

Virginia opossums have 50 teeth. They use their teeth to chew many different kinds of foods.

Opossums are not picky eaters. They eat moths, beetles, and other insects. Opossums like snails, worms, and eggs. Opossums also will eat frogs and snakes. But these animals can move quickly. Opossums cannot always catch them.

Opossums eat fruits and vegetables. Apples and corn are some common foods. Opossums eat persimmons too. Persimmons are a kind of berry.

Opossums use their sense of smell to sniff out foods they like to eat. This young opossum has sniffed out some bittersweet berries.

Opossums often eat carrion (KEHR-ee-uhn).
Carrion are dead animals. Opossums also eat
food scraps that people leave behind.

This opossum is hunting for scraps of food in a garbage can.

Wooded areas have plenty of berries for opossums to eat.

Opossums live in many different places. They live in woods and forests. They live on country farmlands too. The places where opossums live are called habitats (HAB-uh-tats). Opossums find all the foods they need in their habitats.

Chapter 3

Mother opossums look for quiet spots to have babies. Where do mother opossums have their babies?

Opossum Babies

Mother opossums are able to give birth when they are about eight months old. The mothers go to quiet places called dens to have babies.

Mother opossums have their babies in hollow logs, tree trunks, and empty squirrels' nests. The mother opossum lines the spot with leaves. She makes a safe den for the babies.

A hollow log makes a good den for this opossum family.

These tiny pink creatures are newborn opossums.

Mother opossums have many babies at once. One mother might have 20 babies. The group of babies is called a litter.

Newborn opossums are very small. They are only half an inch long. They weigh about as much as a honeybee.

Newborn opossums have no fur. Thin skin covers their bodies. Skin even covers their eyes and ears. Only their noses and mouths are open.

Newborn opossums cannot see or hear.

Newborn opossums must stay close to their mothers. They need to drink their mothers' milk. The milk helps opossums grow bigger and stronger.

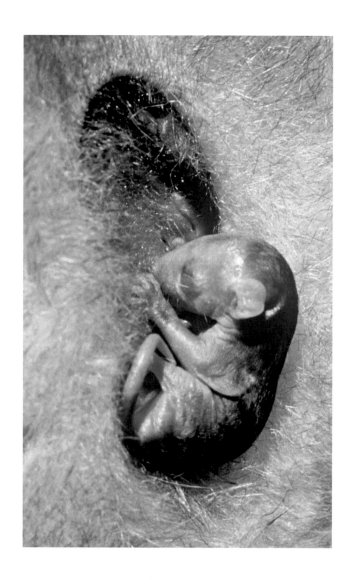

Baby opossums need to drink lots of milk from their mothers.

Baby opossums must climb into their mother's pouch to drink milk. The pouch is called a marsupium (mahr-SOO-pee-uhm). The marsupium is the only place where baby opossums can get milk.

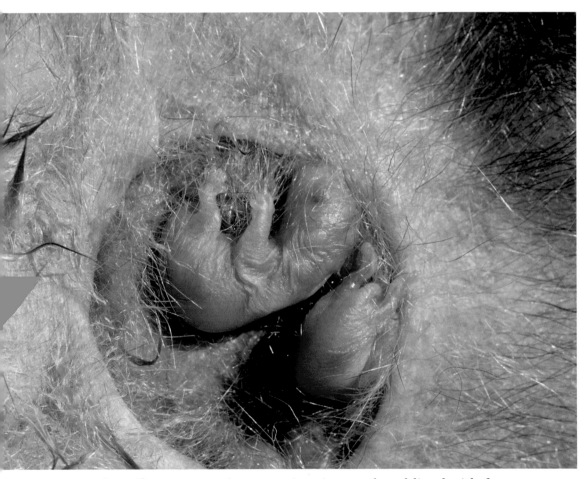

A mother opossum's marsupium is round and lined with fur.

A mother opossum helps her babies reach her marsupium. She licks the fur around the pouch. The babies can smell where their mother has licked. They follow the smell to get to the marsupium's opening.

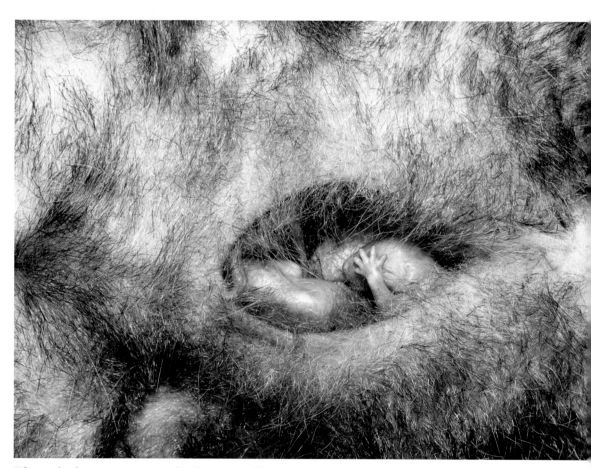

These baby opossums relied on smell to get to their mother's marsupium.

Baby opossums are not very big, but most of them are strong enough to climb to the marsupium.

Newborn opossums use their front legs to get to the marsupium. These legs are very strong. The babies' feet have tiny, sharp claws. The claws help baby opossums drag themselves up to the pouch.

Strong babies make the trip in about one minute. But weaker babies cannot make the trip at all. These babies fall off of their mother's fur. They cannot get to the milk. They do not survive. They are too small to live on their own.

When a mother opossum leaves her den, she carries her babies on her back.

A baby grows quickly inside the marsupium. In one week, it weighs 10 times more than it did at birth. Its tiny claws fall off. New claws grow in their place. The opossum will have these claws for the rest of its life.

Fine hair covers the baby's body. Soon its eyes and ears are open. It begins to poke its head outside the marsupium.

This young opossum is ready to explore the world.

Babies come out of the marsupium when they are about nine weeks old. At first, they stay out for only a short time. They go back into the marsupium to keep warm.

By the time the babies are 11 weeks old, they stay out of the marsupium most of the time. They are ready to explore the world on their own.

Young opossums go with their mother when she hunts for food. Soon the babies learn to hunt for food on their own.

When opossums are ready to explore, their mother begins to wean them. This means she gives them other foods besides her milk. The babies get used to eating other foods. Before long, they no longer need any milk from their mother.

Opossums are fully grown when they are about four months old. They are ready to live on their own. Soon, they will be ready to have their own families.

Young opossums grow up quickly.

Chapter 4

Owls are one of opossums' predators (PREH-duh-turz). What are predators?

Dangers for Opossums

Opossums face many dangers. Owls, foxes, coyotes, and snapping turtles eat opossums. These animals are an opossum's predators. Predators are animals that hunt and eat other animals.

An opossum growls or hisses when it sees a predator. It might show its teeth to scare a predator away. But it doesn't usually fight. Opossums fight only if they have to.

Opossums' sharp teeth can make them look scary. But opossums are usually gentle animals.

An opossum often runs from predators. But opossums do not run fast. Sometimes an opossum cannot get away. If an opossum cannot get away, it has another way of staying safe. It goes completely limp. It falls down on its side. Its body curls slightly, and its tongue hangs out. Predators think the opossum is dead.

Don't be fooled by this opossum! It is not really dead.

If the opossum is lucky, predators will lose interest and leave. Sometimes a predator picks an opossum up and shakes it. Even then, the opossum will not move. It holds perfectly still until the predator goes away.

This dog cannot tell if the opossum is alive or dead. The opossum is holding perfectly still. Opossums can hold perfectly still for up to one hour.

Animal predators are not the only danger for opossums. People can harm opossums too. Opossums often live near people. They live in wooded areas by people's homes.

Opossums sometimes come into people's yards to look for food. This opossum is looking for food near a bird feeder.

Opossums are safest when they stay away from roads.

Sometimes opossums walk on roads where people drive. People in cars may not see the opossums. The animals can be hit by the cars.

Maybe an opossum lives near you!

Cars are very dangerous for opossums. But usually, opossums and people live peacefully together. Since opossums are nocturnal, we rarely see them. And opossums are quiet animals. We may not even know when one is living near our home.

Some night, if you look very closely, you may see an opossum. Notice how its fur gleams in the moonlight. Watch how its feet scurry along the ground.

Opossums sometimes scurry across backyard decks and patios. You might see one if you stay up late at night.

If you're really lucky, you might see a mother opossum with her babies. The opossums will probably disappear quickly into the bushes. Wish the opossums luck on their nighttime hunt.

It's a treat to catch a glimpse of baby opossums. These baby opossums are riding on their mother's back.

Have you ever seen an opossum?

LEARN MORE ABOUT
OPOSSUMS

BOOKS

Fleisher, Paul. *Forest Food Webs.* Minneapolis: Lerner Publications Company, 2008. Learn about the relationships between plants and animals in the forest—a habitat of the Virginia opossum.

Fraser, Mary Ann. *Where Are the Night Animals?* New York: HarperCollins Publishers, 1999. This fun book explores animals that are active at night.

Kalman, Bobbie. *What Is a Marsupial?* New York: Crabtree Publishing Company, 2000. Learn more about opossums and other animals with pouches.

Riley, Joelle. *Koalas.* Minneapolis: Lerner Publications Company, 2006. Read all about the koala, a marsupial that makes its home in Australia.

WEBSITES

Enchanted Learning: Marsupial Printouts
http://www.enchantedlearning.com/coloring/marsupial.shtml
Visit this site to find useful printouts on the Virginia opossum, kangaroo, koala, and other marsupials.

Virginia Opossum
http://www.iwrc-online.org/kids/Facts/Mammals/opossum.htm
Read more about the Virginia opossum at this site.

GLOSSARY

carrion (KEHR-ee-uhn): dead animals. Opossums eat carrion.

dens: the homes in which mother opossums have their babies

habitats (HAB-uh-tats): the places where an animal lives

litter: a group of babies born at the same time to one mother

marsupials (mahr-SOO-pee-uhls): a group of animals that includes kangaroos, koalas, and opossums. Female marsupials have a pouch on their bellies.

marsupium (mahr-SOO-pee-uhm): the name for a mother opossum's pouch

nocturnal (nahk-TUHR-nuhl): active at night

opposable (uh-POH-zuh-buhl) toe: a toe that can hold on to things

predators (PREH-duh-turz): animals that hunt and eat other animals

prehensile (pree-HEHN-suhl): able to wrap around an object. An opossum's tail is prehensile.

wean: to start giving babies other foods besides their mother's milk

INDEX

Pages listed in **bold** type refer to photographs.